30 Part-Time BUSINESS IDEAS ANYONE CAN DO IN 2016

Bonus! - As a way of saying thanks, here's a short book that is guaranteed to excel your business career. It helped me greatly and will do the same for you if you can internalise the concepts.

Download Here → *http://goo.gl/iYx5aC*

Join Our Insider List

Get Our Premium Books Below for Only 99 Cents!

Join Here ^   http://goo.gl/wcNCvW

Insiders get Discounts to our Upcoming Book Titles upon Book Launch.

<u>COMING SOON</u>

30 PART-TIME BUSINESS IDEAS ANYONE CAN DO IN 2016

From a Six Figure Entrepreneur

Written By:

Mateen Soudagar

Brought to you by AffEngineer.com

www.AffEngineer.com Copyright © 2015 by AffEngineer Publishing

Disclaimer

No part of this publication may be reproduced or transmitted in any form or by any means, mechanical or electronic, including photocopying or recording, or by any information storage and retrieval system, or transmitted by email without permission in writing from the publisher.

While all attempts have been made to verify the information provided in this publication, neither the author nor the publisher assumes any responsibility for errors, omissions or contrary interpretations of the subject matter herein.

This book is for entertainment purposes only. The views expressed are those of the author alone, and should not be taken as expert instruction or commands. The reader is responsible for his or her own actions.

Adherence to all applicable laws and regulations, including international, federal, state and local laws governing professional licensing, business practices, advertising and all other aspects of doing business in the US, Canada or any other jurisdiction is the sole responsibility of the purchaser or reader.

Neither the author nor the publisher assumes any responsibility or liability whatsoever on the behalf of the purchaser or reader of these materials.

Any perceived slight of any individual or organization is purely unintentional.

Table of Contents

Introduction

Part time income is one of the most commonly searched topics on the internet. Work, in most cases is enough to pay the bills but doesn't give you that additional income to stay ahead in your finances.

There's nothing less fulfilling then being stuck in a job doing the same thing day in and day out with no plan to exit and live a more financially fulfilling life. Having credit card debts that need to be paid, kids educational expenses, car and house maintenance, food, luxury, holidays, it all ads up to a mountain of costs.

Part time businesses are plentiful BUT there's a catch. For any of the below to work, you WILL need to make it a consistent effort to research and try them and spend a good amount of time getting it off the ground. Sure, the day will come where you just need to spend an hour a day to maintain a healthy part-time income or hopefully even a day where you can quit your day job because of it, but at the starting phase of any business, you need to put in the hours.

Part time business take some time to click but once the process to making money is cracked, it's all down hill from there. Take your time to read through the below ideas and see which one gets you the most excited. Work on that.

1. Blogging

Blogging has been around for a VERY long time. I've been doing it for just over 2 years and my blog makes me a part time income equivalent to most peoples full-time salaries.

I'm not saying it to brag but I'm highlighting the potential of blogging. Some blogs clear a million dollars a year!

Blogging is the process of writing about a certain topic and in time, gathering a following who regularly visit your blog as their interested in what you write.

People have blogs on photography, traveling, entrepreneurship, basically any topic you can think of. How do they make money? They sell ad placements to companies, sell products their affiliated with, use google adsense to monetise ad space, sell ebooks, there's plenty of ways a blogger can earn a living through blogging.

Although it sounds hard, it's not. The term 'website development' might be intimidating but for a person like me who doesn't code, it was very easy to learn. There are tools and programs out there that make creating a website as simple as making a powerpoint presentation. Couple these with plenty of YouTube tutorials on almost anything and you can learn it in a few weekends.

Blogging is a long term play though. I didn't make money for the first full year I was doing it but then again I wasn't monetising my blog at all. Once I started to sell things, I started to make a lot of money from my website.

If you want to get started with this I recommend reading some of the income reports generated by bloggers and seeing if that's the sort of work you'd want to do. I'll list a few below,

http://affengineer.com/income-reports/
http://www.smartpassiveincome.com/my-income-reports/
http://www.matthewwoodward.co.uk/income-reports/

If it is something that interests you, read this post on setting up your blog along with searching, 'wordpress blog tutorial' on YouTube. It might not click immediately which is totally fine. Things will start making sense as you start doing it and working through the hurdles you'll encounter.

It's a long process but can be very fruitful if done right.

2. Ebay

eBay was my business for a long time.

All through university and college, I bought and sold things from different online platforms. Sometimes I would by from eBay and sell it right back on eBay and still turn a profit.

Simple tips like buying from international sellers and re-listing the product as an Australian seller would allow me to make $10 profit off a $5 product!

Ebay is still a gold mine if you spend enough time scouting opportunities. Along with eBay fees make sure you note down postage costs, petrol to and from the post office, materials needed to wrap the product, etc. The more you know about your costs the more money you will make.

You can sell pretty much anything you want on eBay. From books to cars whatever you like. Mind you, just like any other business, it will take you some time to find your sweet spot. I knew a guy who'd make a tonne of cash selling headphones. I sold anything from watches to clothes to pokemon cards. The platform is big enough for everyone.

If your the typeof person that gets a thrill from buying and selling things, ebay might be for you. You can buy products from ebay international sellers, from alibaba.com, garage/yard sales, thrift shops, anywhere really. It's all about experimentation. Set aside a budget you're willing to experiment with. Set aside around $500, see what you can buy with that and try make as much money as you can with that investment.

3. Tutoring

Tutoring can make you a LOT of money.

There's always something you know that something else is willing to pay to learn. It could be something as simple as computer skills or how to cook simple meals. Knowledge is an evergreen niche which is why universities or education in general are some of the biggest industries in the world.

There's a guy who lives a few suburbs away from me that is VERY popular amongst school students. Kids in their final years of school will go to him and pay $15 - $20 per class. He does this in bulk, in a large room he's specifically made for tutoring.

He gets anywhere between 50 – 120 students at a time. If you do the math, that's $750 - $2,400 per 2 hour session and he does about 10 – 15 per week.

Most weeks he'll clear $20,000 easily and that's not even his full-time gig. He's a pharmacist by day so you can imagine how much he makes.

While others were there learning Trigonometry and Algebra, I was there reverse engineering his business model because I was so fascinated in the amount of money he earns.

Tutoring is a big business and parents will pay top dollar if you can provide their children with a valuable learning experience. I'd recommend this method to anyone who's willing to dedicate a couple of hours after work or on the weekends to teach others. Since you know the subjects yourself, you'll enjoy it.

4. Lawn Mowing – Local Services

There are PLENTY of local services to be done in your neighbourhood.

From lawn mowing to weed removal to simple garden trimming, whatever it is, there's always business that can be obtained.

Door-knocking can get you a LOT of business. I know it's intimidating and not what you'd want to do but if you dedicate a couple hours a week knocking on your neighbourhood doors or any neighbourhood for that matter and let them know you're available for specific work.

It can even be carwashing/vacuuming. Whatever people don't have the time to do. The richer the area, the more people are willing to pay for your service so it might be worth it to drive half an hour to work on 2-3 clients that are willing to pay a lot more than your neighbourhood.

Many successful entrepreneurs started off just door-knocking and doing local services. It might even be a great way to teach your kids about entrepreneurship and making money away from the usual mainstream method.

5. Pet Walks

If your a pet lover and an active person, this one is for you!

I get plenty of great ideas form Shark Tank. If you don't know what Shark Tank is, it's a popular show for entrepreneurs who pitch their ideas to investors.

It's exciting and very informative. It gives you insight into the differences between entrepreneurs who have what it takes and people who are just dreamers.

I remember a particular entrepreneur pitching their idea who started off door-knocking while taking his dog for a walk and asking if people wanted their dogs walked too. He'd walk them for a small fee and save people the trouble of having to walk their dog after work.

There are way more lazy people then there are fit so this will always be a viable business idea. Even if you're charging $5 per dog and you take 5 of them per half an hour, that's almost $50 an hour after work!

Do it for an hour or two after work or on the weekends and you'll have a VERY healthy part-time business.

You can even up sell to offer dog grooming/washing/feeding or anything else that comes to mind. Pet people unfortunately don't spend enough time with their pets as they should be giving you a lot of opportunity to make money.

6. Cake Maker

Every now and then I'll receive some fascinating cake design images on my newsfeed from someone with a cake business. Everyone knows someone who has a cake or baking business. It's fulfilling, especially for those who have a hobby and interest for baking.

Simple make a FaceBook Page for yourself, update some of the cakes you've done before and post regularly on some local FaceBook pages. You'll easily get businesses through referrals and family. You can even advertise on Gumtree or Craigslist.

Cake making is a great part time business. A couple of cakes a day can make you over $100 after work. Since you enjoy it, it might not even feel like work and you can make your family something special while your at it too.

7. Gumtree

Gumtree is a wonderland for traders.

Where there are people buying and selling things, there is opportunity to make money so it should come to no surprise that Gumtree is in here.

I know people that make $2-$300+ buying and selling mobile phones. Of course you can buy and sell anything. Never limit yourself to what you know. There could be more profit to be made buying selling wooden chairs or furniture students sell when they leave to go back overseas. You just never know what you will find.

Just like most business ideas here, have a test budget. Say, $500. Using this $500 buy things that you're willing to resell. The beauty about buying selling for profit these days it that there are plenty of markets to work from. By markets, I mean places where people trade. Ebay, Gumtree, local markets are all considered 'markets'.

Some markets have different sell prices for the same product.

My manager used to sell chestnuts during their grow season. He tested a few local markets until he was able to find one where people would buy at a great per kilo' rate. He said some of the guys selling there were just buying from another local market and coming here and reselling the same stock at a slightly higher price.

My cousin just bought a second hand pool table advertised for $450 for $250! He bargained him down almost 50% which is crazy. Just because it's listed a certain price doesn't mean you can't get it cheaper. Chances are, people are willing to drop the price if you can take it off their hands that day or even that hour. You never know peoples financial position.

I once had a rich friend who wanted to get rid of a bunch of his little gadgets. There was an ipod, an LG phone, a TV monitor and few other things. He was willing to sell the whole thing for $500 when at that time, they were worth well over $1,000! I ended up buying it and reselling them for a profit. He wasn't concerned about making money, he just wanted to make enough money back to buy a Nintendo. Again, you never know peoples financial position so always bargain.

List this idea down if you're hobby is buying and selling. Chances are, you've already tried it but take it more seriously, there is definitely potential to make a decent part time income.

8. Baby Sitting/Child Minding/Pick up drop off

My mothers main business is a home daycare service. Sometimes, apart from the usual 9-5 child minding she has to do, she sometimes gets requests to pick up and drop off some school kids.

Sometimes she'll look after them after school for a couple of hours until their parents come pick them up. It's not difficult work. Most of the time, they're hungry from school activities and just want to come home, eat and relax. All she does sometimes is put on their favorite show or give them some drawing papers/textas and let them be busy till their parents come by.

Child minding after school is a great option if your working hours suit it. Here in Australia, it's all regulated. Time sheets are filled out with signatures and everything has to be done right. Keep this in mind when going for this option.

You can also do general baby sitting if you're at university or college. Some parents pay top dollar to put their kids in a child care. If you have some weekdays off, advertise your service on Gumtree and undercut these prices. You'll be saving parents a tonne of money while making good money yourself!

Make sure you check out what the legal requirements are in your state, you don't want to be doing something that's legally not allowed. As long as you're doing things right on paper, you have nothing to worry about.

9. Vending Machines

Vending machines were something I was looking into for a long time. These days you can get all types of vending machines. From the traditional soft drink, chocolate and chips vending machine to machines that charge phones for a couple of dollars.

Even machines that sell full prepped healthy, frozen meals or even soup are available. The vending machine model is interesting. You can either buy these machines individually yourself from either eBay, gumtree, or a recognised vending machine manufacturing company and find a location yourself OR you can buy them packaged with a machine and location from a vending machine franchisor.

The easy way to do it is to find a franchisor who's wiling to sell you these machines along with a location they've negotiated for you. The catch is, they're often MUCH more expensive then doing things yourself. You may end up paying double, sometimes even triple the price doing it this way but it's safer and if it's your first time, it might be the better option.

If you're the risky, "I want to do it myself" type of person then you can try doing it yourself. There's no shortage of vending machines for sale on eBay. If you do a quick search you'll see what I'm talking about. Make sure you know what the vending machine regulations are in the location you wish to set it up in.

I would recommend to call a bunch of places and see what the requirement is to place a vending machine in their area. You may find the government only allows a certain type of vending machine in certain areas. Make sure you know these limitations, (if there are any), before you go ahead and purchase one.

You also have to be prepared to do repairs if the situation requires. Sometimes, the machine will stop taking coins or take coins but not eject a snack. People will complain and maybe even damage the machine. At one of my first jobs, the machine would take coins and not eject snacks way too many times. People would get frustrated and some would even bring in their own snacks and sell them upstairs. Educate yourself on what can go wrong. Google 'vending machine forums' and read threads on people who have had vending machine experiences. Here is a great read. I'm sure there are many more.

10. Garage/Yard Sale Hunting

I did this for a while. Motivated by shows like Antique Trader and Pawn Stars it felt like there was opportunities to make money in places where people didn't know the value of things.

I was right. I would a variety of things people were willing to sell for $20 - $30 that I could easily flip for $120 - $200. I learned a lot about gaming. Many Nintendo consoles were still worth over $200. Even some Nintendo 64 games could be sold for over $300 if you had the case and booklet.

Do an ebay search for the N64 game 'Conkers Bad Fur Day' and see how much money they sell for, you'll be amazed! Some N64 consoles were special edition. They were specific colors, some were themed Pokemon and other promotional themes.

Games like these have give people nostalgia and those willing to pay, will pay good money for them. I purchased a full set of perfect Pokemon cards for almost $200. The guy I bought it off was probably happy with the money but I was happy just knowing I have it.

At a garage sale I bought a broken Playstation 3 for $20. After checking it out on eBay and some playstation forums I realised the one I had bought was a special edition one that was one of the first Playstation 3 releases! It was the only Sony Playstation 3 that would play back games from the previous Sony Consoles and even though it was broken, I was still able to sell it for $140!

Garage sale hunting is exciting and I'm sure if I had continued with it, I could have made a lot more money. Sometimes you'll just find handy items for dirt cheap. Remember, these items are an eyesore for the people selling them as they've been around for years collecting dust. They're just happy you've come along to take it off them. Don't be afraid to bargain.

Make sure you go early. There are plenty of people just like you looking for a bargain. Looking for something they can quickly flip for cash and these people usually come right in the morning. In the first half hour to an hour a lot of the really good stuff is gone.

In saying that, I've come to garage sales at 3pm and still found great items. You just never know what you'll find. The more you search, the more things you find.

Yard/Garage sale hunting is another idea for the buy/sell hobyist.

11. Antique Trading

There's a show called Antique trader that comes on here in Australia in the mornings. It's a show where an antique specialist will go around talking to people who own certain antiques and tell them the value of their item. Some would be worth in the 10s of thousands catching people by total surprise.

There are thousands of items out there that people don't know the value of. From letters passed down from war times to hand made samurai sword sets.

Gold mines are everywhere if you're willing to search for them. Antique trading is a fun hobby, one that teaches you about history. If you're someone that is interested in history then you'll already be ahead of most people.

Items of value are usually hand made by people that have passed away or a set of people that simply don't make the product anymore. The rarer and more sought out the item, the more value it will have. From paintings to books, there is no shortage of things you can find in the antique department.

Give this one a go along with yard sale hunting. With mobile technology you can quickly google the value of things to see if it's worth the buy or not. Technology that many people don't use yet.

12. *Jumping Castle Hire*

I knew a family friend that was in this business. Hiring out party equipment is a great way to make some money. You can even up-sell them on insurance and whole party set ups.

Jumping castles can be bought from a variety of places. From the traditional eBay to looking for a bargain on Alibaba.com, there's no shortage of these. You can get small ones, medium sized ones, castles that are big enough to fit a small classroom of kids, even jumping castles especially themed a certain tv show or disney movie.

At our child care business, all the girls are obsessed with the movie 'Frozen'. If you had a jumping castle with the Frozen movie theme, EVERY girl would want that at her birthday party. Once you get it at one kids party, their friends parents will take note and you'll soon start getting referral business.

Most people have parties on the weekends so the best thing about this business is you can make bookings for upcoming weekends, knowing exactly how much you're going to make. If you're able to hire out 3-4 jumping castles every weekend ranging from $150 - $300 per hire, you can make a great amount of money, sometimes even rivalling your day job.

Remember, it's not just jumping castles here. People hire out Photo booths, sumo suits, Fairy floss machines, all sorts of things! You can easily do a package deal that can make you a lot of money.

13. House Cleaning on Weekends

House cleaning has become a major chore these days for the busy couple. With hardly any free time left outside of work, the last things you want to do is come home and do MORE work.

There is always business opportunity in saving people 1 of two things. Either you can save peoples money by providing a better price on a product or, you're saving them time. Time they don't want to be spending on chores. A cleaning business falls in the latter category.

If you can take this away form people for a decent price, you can make some good money. People in rich areas are willing to pay top dollar for regular quality services and the best things about this business is that it's repeat business. All you have to do is land a few decent clients who order regularly and you'll be guaranteed your income for however many days your contracted on for.

Cleaning often gets a bad rep because it's something that sounds bland and boring not to mention a little third rate. For those who can get past this mentality and see it as a business opportunity, there is plenty of money to be made.

I used to have a friend who's father had a cleaning business. They had a small team of cleaners who would do the work, all they had to do was manage employees and find work.

A cleaning business can vary from simple cleaning and

vacuuming of houses and domestic properties to full scale bathroom and carpet steam cleaning. You decide what you're willing to provide and take it from there.

Remember, with every business venture you want to start, you HAVE to have a marketing plan. It could be as simple as door knocking 20 houses a day or facebook marketing. Whatever you decide to do, make an excel spreadsheet and list the techniques you're going to use. From there, go through each one and note down the results and figure out which technique works the best. Focus on this to expand your cleaning business.

Lastly, at the start, you'll have to provide something better than what's currently out there. You have to be willing to go that extra mile and treat your customers like gold, give them a great experience, have great pricing and generally be an ideal service for someone who requires cleaning. Once you start getting more business, you can always change these around but it's always the businesses that provide exceptional value that become the most successful.

14. Instagram/Facebook

Instagram and FaceBook are social media websites that spread through the world like a virus. They've both grown rapidly and both fall under the same company since Instagram now owns FaceBook. The question is, how do we make money from?

There are plenty of ways. Facebook is my bread and butter. I've spent over 150k on their advertising platform so I definitely know a thing or two on where opportunities lie.

Instagram and FaceBook are different in the way they provide value to their user base but essentially work the same way. You have an account about yourself, you post things, people who know you become connected to your profile and do the same, you continue posting things and engaging with everyone around you.

The above is what happens with most personal FaceBook and Instagram account but what about FaceBook pages? What's the point of having them and how exactly are they making money from having one?

FaceBook Pages and Instagram Business accounts work on gathering a readership. They'll grow a readership in a particular niche, posting valuable content, videos and images and slowly growing to a considerable number. Once they're at over 50-100k+ fans, they'll be contacted by people who would like to promote things on their page.

For example. This kindle book is about entrepreneurship. There are many entrepreneurship related FaceBook and Instagram pages. If I were able to pay $20 - $50 to each related page/account I found to post a picture and link to my book on Amazon, wouldn't that be valuable to me? I might spend $500 reaching about 1 million+ people! The page admins would receive a small fee for just posting a simple update on their pages and I'll receive exposure of my product/service/brand. A win win.

There are Instagram accounts earning over $2-300 a day doing this. They started off just making an Instagram account about a particular topic and every day posting 3-5 pictures with as many relevant hashtags as possible. Liking and Following as many related fans as they possibly could so they could like them back. 6 months to a year later they'll have a page getting contacted like crazy for marketing opportunities.

The next time you see a niche Instagram account posting a nice picture of a holiday resort or a Mercedes Benz, visit their page and you'll notice a 'contact admin for business' email. This is how they get contacted for business opportunities.

This might be something for people with busy work schedules who can use their phones to update their Instagram accounts. I have a few accounts I'm currently growing. I haven't started monetising it yet but I know their time will come.

15. Simple Catering Business

We used to own a small catering business a while ago. My family is from India and we're big on butter chicken and biryani. I mean, who isn't!? There are plenty of indians here in Melbourne so we decided to partner up with a family friend and start a small catering business.

We'd get orders to make Biryani and curries and all sorts of things. We'd spend a weekend making the food and sell it for a great price. We just did this for a select few foods and for mostly people that were of indian ethnicity. Imagine how much potential there is for foods of other types?

If you're good at making food from a particular country and you love doing it, this one could be for you. If we were to have started the business again, I would have made a FaceBook page regular posting our happy customers and orders all over FaceBook. Business would have been a lot more as most of my family friends are from the asian subcontinents.

These days with free promotional tools like FaceBook, Instagram and gumtree, there is a lot of potential for businesses like these. If you can get a bit creative with your pictures and are willing to put yourself out there, this business can quickly replace your full-time job.

There are plenty of birthdays/weddings/religious events/random events happening on any given day, all you need is a few orders a week and it will keep you plenty busy.

16. Juicing/Healthy Food

One of the largest growing industries in the world is the health foods industries. As more and more people are realising that the foods they eat provide little to no nutritional value, they're looking for more healthier options. Some people take their health VERY seriously.

I've been experimening with a bunch of diets for a long while now. From going 100% raw fruits and vegetables to paleo to currently fruits and vegetables only, (cooked or raw), I feel great and hope one day will be able to permanently transition to this diet.

The problem is, healthy food takes so long to make! You need to juice, blend, grind, cut, peel, clean, etc etc. Way too much for someone like me who works for himself. I spend 1-2 hours a day just making my meals and buying my fruits and veggies. Sometimes I think it would be bloody great if someone could do some of these tasks for me.

Another problem is sourcing purely organic foods. Most of the stuff you see at the market has been chemically sprayed, polished, waxed, you name it. I've had apples last a whole month STILL looking shiny and fresh. Something's terribly wrong there. Purely organic fruits and vegetables are very healthy and are hard/expensive to find. If you can find them cheap and make some great juices, smoothies, snacks, I'd be your first customer.

Healthy raw food places are VERY expensive here in

Melbourne. It will cost you $15 - $20 for a plain salad in the city, sometimes up to $12 for half a litre of juice!

I often see small businesses in shopping centres selling healthy juices in a bottle, (which I'm convinced have had water added to it in order to dilute and sell more), with a massive line in front selling juice to hundreds of people a day. Even in India, healthy fresh juice places are becoming very popular at food joints.

If you're big on healthy food, this could be a great business idea for you. The expansion potential is HUGE and you can advertise all over FaceBook and Gumtree. Not only that but you can charge premium prices for them since people are willing to pay top dollar for healthy, organic food. Do some research and see what you find. It doesn't take long to learn some simple healthy juice and smoothie recipes.

17. Freelancer Designer

When someone thinks design they think of someone that has gone to design school, has a massive portfolio of amazing artwork and have been immersed in artful activities since they were a child. Sure, this is how it worked traditionally where you had to stand out in an interview with your love for art and superior talent but not so much anymore.

These days people need all sorts of designs made. From small intro videos to a a youtube video to phone app logos to website templates, there are plenty of jobs online if you have a look.

If you live in the western countries and speak good english, you have an advantage. Most of the work I outsource, I give to people in the west or who can speak great english. I've tried to go with the cheaper countries but when communication is a problem, work gets done at a ridiculously slow pace, especially with work that falls in the design category. Communicating design ideas requires a lot of understanding between both parties.

Go to www.elance.com and search 'design'. See what jobs come up. If you're interested, make a profile and bid on the work. Learn some photoshop, there are plenty of YouTube tutorials going around. It took me a few weekends to get to an intermediate level so I could design my Phone app screens. If you're serious about anything, you'll be surprised how fast you can teach it to yourself.

A quick search on elance gives me the following jobs,

"Hi, I need someone to match the green in our main logo with the blue in our shortened "DB" logo. The blue in DB should be the color green in our main font. Should't take more than a few minutes but they must be matched appropriately."

"I am looking for a Graphic Designer who knows how to design informational reports and guides. We have about 10 to do on a monthly basis.

Each guide will be submitted to you in a Google doc format. You will be provided a colour scheme and/or logo if it is available. The reports are between 2,000 and 5,000 words on average."

Like this, there are plenty of jobs at any given time. Make an effort, take a small risk and try bid on some work. You have nothing to lose than an opportunity. All it takes a few jobs a week to earn a decent income and if you're able to land a permanent client, you might be able to cut down on your full-time job!

18. Freelancer Developer

Developing is a skill not many people know. And for people that don't know, they are too intimidated by coding to try learn it. If you know some simple coding, whether through school or your profession, there is ample opportunity for you guys.

Coding has become more and more simple due to programs out there making the process easier for people like me. Whether it's wordpress or wysiwig, there's a lot of tools out there that can make amazing designs in less than an hour. My blog template looks great and I continuously receive all sorts of compliments for it.

What most people don't know is that it took me less than an hour to do! All I did was select a free template on wordpress, changed the color themes and I had a beautiful blog ready to work on.

People would easily pay $100 to get something like this. Wordpress allows you to make even more complicated websites just as easily. Websites that look like jobseek.com or even merchant websites like Amazon. There are templates that suit almost every need which, if you can learn to install and customize slightly, will be VERY impressive to prospective clients.

You can find work similar to the design topic before this one. Eg, via elance or you can even cold call/email companies in your local directory of a mockup design for their website and how much you'd charge for it.

The best thing about this type of work is that, they'll need someone to continuously monitor the website and make little updates and edits here and there. The obvious choice would be to go with you if you can provide a fair price. This leaves the doors open to more up-sells and all sorts of things!

Wordpress is another tool that can be learned over a few solid weekends. Youtube is filled with Wordpress Tutorials so take a look and see if it's for you!

Nevertheless, it's a great skill to have under your belt as eventually you'll require your own website to be built. If you can save 2-5k building your own simple website over outsourcing it, you can spend that money on marketing and obtaining customers which can make the difference between success and failure for your business.

19. Freelancing in General

I've only covered 2 of literally 1000s of different freelancing jobs you can do. From solving math problems for struggling university students to offering professional Civil Engineering advice, there is really no limit to the types of jobs you can do apart from any you have to physically be there for.

Freelancing has opened the doors do ample opportunity and there are many that are still not aware of websites like elance.com. Yes, there may be some competition but if you can stand out and get the ball rolling with some work then you can start to get some consistent work.

If I ever had to start entrepreneurship from scratch, I'd probably start with this strategy. Mostly because you can literally bid on 100s of projects in a day if you really dedicate yourself to finding work. This is equivalent to door-knocking 100 houses which is VERY effective in the business world.

And also for the fact that it is massively scaleable. If you start becoming one of the top providers of a particular service you can start hiring employees and slowly expanding your offshore company. There are many companies or individuals on elance that have provided more than a million dollars worth of work! I know someone who runs a company and has generated over 1 million dollars worth of client income off elance.

He has a small team of people which he gets work for.

Nothing fancy, they all work in a small office with basic equipment but they get the work done which is the main thing.

If you haven't done it yet, go over to elance.com, create a profile and click 'Find Work'. Go through jobs and see if there's anything you're interested. Some work I can find right now,

QUICK CA$H for: CREATIVE ROMANCE WRITERS!
Blog for my special water bottle
Blog/Article Content Writing, Editing, and Optimizing
OCTOBER ARTICLES ON VARIOUS TOPICS FOR A COMMUNITY NEWSPAPER
Write Content & Branding for a Retail Website
Business blogger
Recipes writer
Resume Re-edit

There were another 700 jobs available!

Not to mention more updated every day. It's almost a guaranteed work for you to find additional income, it's just a matter of you following through and finding some work.

In fact all of the tactics in this book can be achieved. It's really just our ind that is the limit to whether you'll be successful or not. The person that makes it is the one that believes in himself and pushes through that doubt to the point they give these ideas a fair shot. It's a patient and long journey and you have to be willing to motivate yourself to get your feet moving.

20. Mobile Phone/Tech Repairs

Almost everyone I know who's ever owned a smart phone has at some point had a cracked screen or foggy camera or some little annoying issue that needed to be fixed. As consumers we don't really questions the workings of our technology, most of us use it and are happy just knowing how it can be used in our day to day lives.

If you've ever had an issue with your phone and tried to fix it yourself, you would have seen plenty of youtube videos going through mobile phone issues and fixes. Not only that but most of these fixes are simple and can be done by buying the necessary replacement parts off of eBay for a lot less than the price then people are willing to pay for someone to fix it.

If you find technology being something you enjoy reading into then this might be for you.

The other day my brothers Playstation 4 had an issue where one of his game discs got stuck and you couldn't eject the disc tray. This effectively made the Playstation useless and I know plenty of people that would have just bought a new one at this point. Dad is very mechanically minded and he loves fixing small things like this so he thought he'd give it a shot.

He pulled out his iPad and went through a few youtube videos. He found out that in most cases it's the rollers under the tray that come off their plastic holders. They simply need to be popped back in or if broken, replaced. He spent a couple of days researching, buying the necessary parts and fiddling around with the Playstation to get it fixed and working again. It cost us less than $5 and some time. My brother was quoted $60 just to find out what was wrong with the problem and most likely another $100+ to go ahead with a fix.

Screen repairs here can cost a minimum of $140 - $200 and in most cases their just a screen replacement which can be done for less than $50. It's a delicate process and it might take you a few tries to get it right but after some time fiddling with second hand broken phones, you'll know how to fix a variety of problems.

With technology becoming more lighter and more capeable, it seems they're also becoming more fragile. This is an opportunity for us to find a solid part-time income if needed.

I remember when I had a Playstation 2 issue and took it to the market to get quoted, there was a line of people wanting to get quotes for their little gadgets and gizmos. The couple of guys working there had a bunch of playstations in the queue and were already filled with work. I wouldn't be surprised if they were making more than $1,000 a day doing it!

There are plenty of broken phones you can buy on ebay. It would be a good investment to buy a few of these and try fix them. You can always resell them and recover your money buy putting them back on eBay if all else fails. There is no better way to educate yourself then to jump right in and start doing the work. This doesn't just apply to this strategy but all strategies mentioned in this book. Short courses and things are great to learn the basics but if you can do dummy projects with a limited budget, you'll find yourself learning tonnes more.

21. Kindle Publishing

This book is only available via Amazon Kindle so if you're reading this, you would have definitely got it from there. Have you ever wondered how much authors like me make doing this?

You'd be surprised how easy it really is to publish something on Kindle. Anyone can do it, you don't need a qualification or decades of experience in the topic you're writing about, you just need knowledge that you KNOW is valuable to others. I've earned over 300k in revenue in the last couple of years working for myself and my mindset has done a complete 180 since quitting work so I know what's required to start becoming financially independent. I could have waited for the day I was a millionaire to release a book like this but I didn't need to. Like I said, ANYONE can start writing.

Education is a huge industry and people are prepared to pay a good amount of money for valuable information. I have a set of book and video courses on my blog that I was selling for $127 at one stage. People bought them and I'm yet to have someone say something negative or return the product even though I have a 100% money back guarantee policy!

That's just one of my side businesses I have that I experiment with. I used it to see how much I could push the price and still get people to buy. I've been in courses that were over $1,000! Education is a huge industry and everyone has some advice to offer. From over coming depression to finding a job in your specific career, there are plenty of things you can write about.

You may be thinking that 'writing is not really my thing' and I don't blame you. I can only think of a handful of books I've read in my whole 26 years. My worst subject by far at school was english and essays and theory assignments were a nightmare for me.

The only difference now is that I actually know what I'm talking about. When you know what you're talking about then words flow off your fingers like butter spreads on hot toast. It's almost effortless and as you're writing you start to understand more about yourself.

I'm almost at 200 blog posts on my blog which is huge for me considering how much I never thought I'd have a career in writing.

Just to give you an idea of the earning potentials, I know people making over $40k a month off their kindle sales. People have become millionaires off kindle and started massive brands and businesses off their books. The best thing about it is once you put it up on Kindle Amazon, it's available to the whole world. Anyone can purchase it from any country in the world!

In saying that, don't think it's as easy as just writing something and publishing it on kindle, that's actually the easy part. To drive sales and downloads of your kindle publication, you'll need to do some active marketing and promotion so Kindle can identify it as having some value. Once Kindle starts to pick it up and coupling it other products, listing it on their top sellers lists and generally promoting your book for you, that's where the gold is.

If you ever go down this path. Choose something your passionate about and write a few books in it. Read up on how to promote your kindle book and give it a shot.

Kindle publishing can be a great passive income as your book stays on the store till you or Amazon decide to take it off for whatever reason. A book you wrote last year can STILL be making you money two years down the track! It's one of the biggest reasons I'm experimenting with Kindle Publishing. Passive income opportunities are definitely here.

22. Making Phone Apps

Phone apps were a HUGE opportunity when they first became popular. The iPhone revolutionised the world in many different ways and phone applications were one of the biggest new additions to the mobile scene. Maybe the idea of them had been used before but the way iPhone made them available to the world was never done before.

Instantly there were phone app creators making millions in a matter of months from a simple app such as a torch. What makes the industry so fruitful is the fact that just like kindle, the apps are available to the world.

Phone apps were my first venture and I made a few of them. I always start off the first few ideas in a particular venture as a 'test' to see what works and what doesn't. I made my first app for $200. It was 2 screens and a very simple functionality. I sold them for $5 a pop just to see if anyone would buy them and they did! Some days I sold 2 or 3, most days I sold just 1 but I quickly made my money back and then some after some time.

Just like kindle, publishing a phone app onto the app store is relatively simple. Whether it's Apple or Samsung, the process is relatively the same. You don't even have to know how to code or write programs, my apps were outsourced on elance. I received some local quotes for around $2k-$3k which I thought was crazy for a 5 hour job.

The phone app industry forced me to learn Photoshop so I

could communicate my idea to my developers. I paid between $300 - $800 for my other apps which took just a few weeks to make. As an app publisher all you're really doing is coming up with the idea and going back and forth with the dummy app till your happy with how it all works. That's really all there is to it.

It might be a whole 10 years+ since the iPhone came out but there is still ample opportunity. I here about new apps almost every day. You don't need something as big as angry birds to make a lot of money. There are plenty of apps making a killing that barely anyone has heard of before.

The app industry works similar to kindle in that you need to get your app downloads rolling with some clever marketing and get it to move up in charts. As this happens, more and more people will download your app further increasing them in the charts. If you can get your app in the 'best paid apps' section or 'app of the day' that's when your app will spike and where most people make their money.

Once you get the hang of making phone apps whether via hiring a developer or making them yourself you can start making phone apps for little businesses. There are plenty of phone app development programs out there that make it very easy to make simple phone apps. A restaurant for example would love a simple phone app that lets them update their menu and stay in contact with customers with deals and promos. You can make some dummy apps and cold call restaurants charging them a healthy 2-5k to make a phone app like this.

Phone apps are like websites in that they need regular maintenance to keep running. Small bug fixes, updates to menus and contacts, details and information and general changes here and there are necessary which provide more business opportunity. In this case you can get clients on a monthly fee to provide regular maintenance and data reports. Anything that provides value to your client, you can charge them for.

Companies and business that have been operating for many years really have no time to properly investigate technology. Having you come along and showing what you can do for them with mobile app technology is what they need. It's up to you to sell it as you please and charge them as you wish. You can sell it as an app that improves customer engagement and imporves social sharing ultimately increasing customers. They'll have the app for ever and you can do a small value provision calculation for them. For example, if you charge them $5,000 for the development of the app, technically they need to be able to make that $5,000 up and then some through the app. You can show them how this can be achieved, approximate time frames, etc.

This strategy is almost purely a numbers game. List down all the restaurants in your local are, contact whoever is in charge and show them what you can do for them. Call literally 100 restaurants over the course of a few days. Even if your conversion rate is 5% with an approximate Phone app development charge of $3,500, that's $17,500! That's without even taking a monthly fee into consideration.

I would recommend phone app development for everyone. It taught me the necessary skills to be able to run a 6 figure business. From simple Photoshop design to getting comfortable outsourcing tasks on elance to understanding the importance of good marketing. By the end of the process you will learn tonnes about business which is where the real value is.

23. Car Boot Sale/Yard Sale

This ties in with the yard sales, eBay and Gumtree idea.

There's at least $1,000 worth of things in my room I can think of that I would be happy to sell at the right price. For a while now I've been putting off the task of holding a yard sale and selling them off. From old painting to furniture to phones that are still useable but we just don't use them.

Not to mention how much of your house can be cleaned out during the process. Everyone would be able to do this but it takes a little courage to go through your house and make a serious decision on whether or not you need a particular item or not.

Often we get caught up thinking that we'll 'use it someday'. That 'someday' rarely comes and all we're left with is a bunch of random items that are placed in the corners of everywhere and simply taking up unnecessary space.

The other day I went though my closet and put everything I haven't worn in the last 3 months into a big plastic bag and donated it to charity. Even if I liked the piece of clothing, the fact that I haven't worn it for the last 3 months shows that I have better choices and these clothes may have been a good buy then but right now, they're jus taking up space.

When we held a yard sale, we spent a full day before

advertising. You can't just put up a couple of signs out side your house and expect people to find it unless you live on a street with heavy traffic. We went to major intersections within a 2km radius around our house and put up clear cardboard signs advertising our yard sales. It was a great turn out and we sold a lot of stuff. There's a few websites out there that will allow you to advertise your yard sale as well not to mention Gumtree and Craigslist.

There are plenty of local markets that you can go to and sell your stuff. One mans junk is another mans treasure and you never know what will be of value to someone else. Do a local search for car boot sales and local markets and note them down on a list. Go to a few of them and note down how busy they are, the type of people that go there and which one would be the best value for money. Remember, you'll have to most likely pay for a spot.

The way this ties into the other business strategies in this book is that everyone has a bunch of things they no longer need that are valuable to others. Simply put, everyone should be able to make at least $500 - $1,000 selling these items. This is a GREAT starting budget to attempt the other ideas mentioned in this book!

If you find it hard to put aside your income from your full-time job, I'd suggest holding a yard sale and selling as many items as you can. Take that money and use it as your experimental budgets when trying out ideas. This way, you'll be more willing to sell things in your house as they're being recycled into business opportunities! If you're smart with your money you can do a lot with it.

Remember, invest small, in ways that still let you learn a lot. Don't buy a bulk pallet of mobile phones for $10,000 until you've sold a good amount yourself and have proven to yourself that your business model works.

24. Social Media Assistant

This one is similar to the Phone App idea for businesses. One of the best businesses to be in right now is the online industry. There's always billions of dollars moving through the space at any given time, it's just a matter of getting a piece of that pie.

Social Media is word given tremendous value to businesses over the recent decade. Businesses hear about it everywhere, they KNOW they should be doing something about it but just don't have the time to step away from their business and create and maintain an account. Maintaining a social media account is no easy task. You need to constantly take pictures, schedule posts, respond to messages and comments, it needs your constant attention.

The beauty of this business is that there are just so many social media possibilities and every year or two another giant gets introduced to the scene. The current major players are Pinterest, Instagram, FaceBook and Twitter. You can provide to set and manage all these at a fee and again, there are ample businesses that will be happy to pay for this if you can show them the value of it.

Don't be afraid of charging in the thousands. Yes, they're not hard to make but if managed right can provide tremendous value to the businesses your making them for. They bring them repeat customers, let them reach-out to more customers and provide a communication channel between the business and their locality that can keep there business constantly ticking. Marketing is a huge part of a successful business and anyone that has been in business for a while knows the importance of great marketing and keeping in touch with customers.

I would employ the quantity strategy here again. List out 100 restaurants or businesses your interested in. Make a couple of dummy apps for dummy businesses you can send over to them as a sample and see how many and at what rate you convert. Again, a 5% conversion rate means you'l get 5 clients which is all you need for a decent part time income. To get more clients, all you need to do is call more businesses. It's such a powerful strategy and should never be underestimated.

Over time, you can employee people to cold call for you and even develop the product. You can hire a salesman to go over and pitch the product and basically automate the business.

If you're tech savvy, this is a great opportunity. You can bundle it up with making them a website and a phone app and charge them a package deal. You're doing a LOT for them and charging $10,000 for all this is actually quite cheap.

I was quoted $3,200 for a small app that cost me $200 to develop. People are willing to pay any dollar if you can convince them that this amount is worth the value you provide. It's the reason top salesman's make a killing.

25. Photography/Wedding Photography

Photography has been around for ages. From what started as portrait drawings in the 1800s have now become huge business opportunities for the savvy entrepreneur. Clever filtering apps and simple Photoshop apps make picture taking a breeze. Not to mention smartphones auto filtering for you that make even the most simple pics look like they've been taken by a professional.

I've been approached a few times by people wanting to provide picture portraits of my car. They've left a card with a business name and I can imagine people with good cars saying yes. People love certain things that they possess and a picture is a way to eternally capture a moment that brings back nostalgia again and again.

Whether it's Cars or Weddings. A Photography business is great to get into. People need photographers for Birthdays, Weddings, Funerals, Functions, Graduation days, you name it. You can easily land a photography gig for a couple hundred dollars over the weekend, in many cases much more.

I have a friend who has a businesses that provides photography and video recording services for weddings. He started off doing it as a hobby more than 5 years ago. Now it's his main business and earns him over 100k per years. The best thing about it is it's almost completely automated. He'll send out a couple of employees that know how to talk and connect with clients on the day. They'll return back with photos and videos of the day. My friend will spend a day putting it all together on a CD or USB which he'll post out in the mail.

To lock him in they need to pay 50% of the cost upfront which is a minimum $1,500. People like to book their wedding plans in a year or more in advanced so he'll be paid out in the 10s of thousands before he even does the job!

Opportunities like his are endless and if you can prove to provide a great, happy service and people enjoy having you around, your sure to get referral business. Visually appealing businesses like these are also great in terms of social media advertising. You can have a Facebook, Pinterest and Instagram account that regularly updates people with your work kind of acting like a portfolio for potential clients. All you need is a few clients to flood your account with some pictures. You'll need to get a little creative with marketing after that and provide special deals at the start to get the business off it's feet.

It's always better to focus on one thing. Don't have a photography business that focusses on everything because you won't become the 'go to guy' for anything. Business need to stand out and to do so it's sometimes best to become the best in the business at one thing.

It's better do be known as the guy that provides photography services for specifically European cars then it is to be known for someone that provides photography services for everything That way you'll stand out and will be able to dominate that specific market.

Put yourself in the clients position. If you wanted someone to repair you iphone would you go to someone who has a general tech repair business or to someone that specialises in iPhone repairs? Obviously the latter because they'll know the ins and outs of the phone since it's all they deal with. In Business it's better to be the master of something then the jack of all trades, at least at the start. Once your business grows, you can experiment with different parts of the industry but for now, pick something your interested in and start providing that service.

26. Flipping Cars

I'm not referring to flipping cars like the Hulk. I'm referring to the business of buying and selling cars. I've been interested in flipping cars for as long as I can remember, I've just never had the money to do it. And when I DID have the money to do it, there were better opportunities I decided to spend my time on. Nevertheless, for the technical minded, this is and will always be a fruitful industry.

I did give this a shot once. I purchased a 2002 Toyota Supra for $5,000. The car was in great condition and was my friends neighbours. My friend is the very definition of car maniac. If every you find that in the dictionary, you'll probably see his face next to it. He saw this as a great business opportunity and said the car was worth a lot more then that and it's an easy $1k each if we do this. So I agreed and invested my $5k. A couple of weeks later it was sold for $8k and we made a cool $1.5k each. That's one of the easiest ways I've made money. I decided to focus on other things but my friend now works with another guy buying and selling cars for profit together.

One will find the cars, invest and drop the car off at my friends. And he'll list it and get it sold splitting the profits among himself and his investor.

The idea here is to buy REAL cheap. These guys get cars worth $8,000 for $2,000. They'll bargain hard on Gumtree, Craigslist, CarSales, other online websites. They'll go to auctions and try pick up a bargain. There's never been a time my friend has told me a price he paid for a car that I haven't dropped my jaw in amazement. I guess you never know how desperate people are to sell their car and so never feel scared lowballing them.

You can never know everything that's wrong with a car which is why buying cheap is the main part of the process. Accounting for the financial risks of finding problems here and there is what will ensure you profit the majority of the time. Don't just look to buy a car $500 cheaper then what you think you can sell it for. Remember, you also may have to pay for things that go wrong with the car, registration, stamp duty, taxes & fees, towing costs, petrol, cleaning and detailing, etc. Make a list of common costs and make sure you're accounting for this cost when purchasing a car to flip.

Depending on the car make, there's a general price of parts you will start to learn about. For example Fords and Holdens here in Australia are quite common so finding replacement parts at the wreckers is no bid deal and is quite inexpensive. Same thing with most Hondas, Toyotas and Nissans. If you've got yourself something a little rarer. Maybe an Old Mercedes or a BMW, you'll find yourself paying more for replacement parts.

If I need to replace the whole engine and transmission for a 2000 Honda Civic, (worst case scenario), it'll probably cost me $800 but if I needed to do the same for a 2000 Mercedes or BMW it would probably cost me around $2,000. Be wary of what you purchase. Do some research on forums and websites for how much replacement parts generally cost and pay what you think is a ~~good~~ great price.

If you're going to try this strategy I'd suggest to start small. It's easy to get excited and put all your savings in your first buy to maximise your profits but you have to account for the fact that this is your first try and most likely you'll make mistakes along the way. The trick here is to make mistakes and learn from them without losing money you can't afford to lose. Worst case scenario you will sell the car for a lot less then what you bought it. It could cost you a lot if you purchased an expensive car and it turned out to be a lemon.

Start small and buy cars that are inexpensive to fix. This is different depending on where you buy it. Here in Australia Nissan Pulsars, Honda Civics, Honda Accords, Toyota Camry's and other 4 Cylinder makes that are known to be tough are good buys. Parts are cheap and mechanics are plentiful. Start with these, spend $2-$3k or whatever is ok for you to trial with.

Over time, just like anything else here it's a numbers game. Call 10-20 cars for sale on Gumtree and try bargain with them. You're sure to get a great deal eventually if you keep this process. You'll get better as you go so don't be disheartened if you don't make as much money as you thought you would. In Business you will make money and you WILL lose money. It's a fact of business. Take losses as they come, learn from them and don't ever make the same mistake twice.

27. Stock Investing

Stock Investing was the first financial industry I was ever interested in as a kid. I still remember sitting on my dads lap being 8 years old and logging in for him while he closed his eyes and telling him whether it was a red arrow or a green arrow next to his stock. Red indicating it's gone down and green indicating it's gone up.

Later on during university I decided to invest my own money in stock and learn it myself. I invested $10,000 in Telstra shares which our Australias main telecommunications provider and it immediately went down 10-15% over the next few weeks. I kept my money in there and by the end of the year it was up 20%. I took my money out and was grateful to have learned to track trends and understand how the share market works.

I had also received dividends which are semesterly payouts, (they kind of work like bonuses), on stock you've invested in. Big companies share their profits with investors and pay them out as 'dividends'. If I had 5,000 shares with Telstra at $2 a piece and they paid out 10 cents per dividend every semester then every six months I'd receive a check for $500.

People make money many ways in stock. You can leave your money in there and make money as the value of the company and consequently your stock price increases. You can leave it in there and make money through dividend payouts. If you're smart with this you might be able to get a stock at a great price and return 10% per annum in just dividends which is more than twice as much as the banks interest deposits. OR you can even day trade which is basically buying and selling different stock throughout the day for profits. It's a great way to learn but extremely stressful as you're making and losing money all day.

I would recommend picking a few stock in different companies, looking and their past data and investing a small amount in each. This way you force yourself to learn about the industries you've invested in and basically force yourself to become more wary of business opportunities.

Stock investing is the lazy mans way of making money. You can buy and sell from your phone app which is what I do. I remember being over seas and my stock investment went up 35% in one day! I cashed out and made a few thousand dollars just that day.

My dad once told me a story of a guy that used to work with him. The stock that he had invested in, he bought when they first listed themselves on the stock exchange. When a company first goes public, meaning they decide to list themselves for the very first time on the stock exchange making them available to seek outsider investors like me, they release their stock at a set price. The market then determines how much this stock rises and falls throughout it's career on the stock exchange. Anyway, the guy had bought them very early and for well under a dollar. After about 5-10 years they had risen almost 50 fold and his 50k investment had increased to 2-3million.

I'm sure that's the story that had my dad hooked on the stock market. It's also the story that keeps me dreaming for something like that.

Nowadays I don't leave much money in the bank. It's either in paypal ready to be used for my online business or in stock. Yes, I keep some money in the bank as back up but the more money you have out there working for you, the more you're going to learn about opportunities.
Making big money has a lot of luck behind it but you can increase your chances of luck by positioning yourself in areas where luck can get to you.
A surfer would never catch a big wave unless he buys himself a surfboard, learns to surf and floats around areas where waves are massive. Business is the same. Put yourself in places where booms happen and hope that one will get to you throughout your lifetime.

28. Custom Clothing

Custom Clothing is where I made my small fortune. Enough to last me a couple years in business with a healthy monthly spend budget to learn from.

The Custom Clothing and Merchandise industry has become huge over the years upon the introduction and growth of websites like Etsy and Teespring. They provide a platform to showcase your products where people can buy from you.

Go to Etsy.com and all the products you see on that site are made by someone like you who has a small workshop in their room, garage, home and fulfil orders as they get them. If your the crafty type that make a few things, list them on Etsy and do some basic marketing. Depending on what your selling it can quickly grow into a full-time business.

Etsy also have an affiliate program which allow people in my core profession, (affiliate marketing), to promote your product for you for a 5% commission. If someone knows how to market your product right you can get a huge boost of sales spiking your business and permanently increasing orders. This is one of the reasons companies like Etsy and Amazon became so big. They're affiliate program made almost every online entrepreneur a marketing machine and they promoted these businesses like crazy.

Teespring is another business that works similar to Etsy. Similar but not the same.

Unlike Etsy, you don't make or buy the product. In fact you never physically see the product. You just create it by designing the prints for the merchandise you're willing to sell. Merchandise can be in the form of Phone Covers, Hoodies, Shirts, Caps, Bags and all sorts of things.

You have to come up with the design and market it. When you bring in sales, Teespring will go get it printed and ship it to the customer for you. You don't deal with the customer or fulfilment of the product. All you do is design the product and bring in sales. That's all. Although it seems like easy work, it's a lot harder. Marketing isn't easy but doing this will teach you how to get better at it.

I decided to focus on Teespring for all of 2014. I made a lot of money doing it, over 6 figures but the most important thing was it taught me how to utilise the internet to bring in sales for your online business. Having an online store set up with products ready to go is the easy part. Anyone can do that but getting consistent sales, growing a customer base and nurturing them so they become return visitors is where the real gold is. If you can do this part, you've proven to yourself you can run a successful business.

I would suggest to read up on some Teespring threads and forums. I have a bunch of free tutorials available to anyone on my blog. They're broken down into 2-5 minutes and are easy to go through. See what you think.

29. Growing and Selling Produce

My manager at the last job I ever worked in used to have a chestnut farm he'd harvest every once a year. Him and his wife would drive down there, spend a few days picking and cleaning chest nuts. Then come down here and sell them at local markets.

It was a cool 10k, (I'm sure it's more now), and he'd have sold most through pre-orders before even going ahead and picking them. He's chestnuts would sell like hot cakes as they were great quality, freshly picked and at a great price.

With the health food industry on the rise as people become more aware of the benefits of healthy eating, there are ample people looking for clean, fresh, organic food to buy from. If you have a good sized back yard that can grow these foods and love gardening, this is a good idea to implement.

You can mix it up selling fresh juices and smoothies along with fresh produce. Ideas like these work well because most potential customers search free classified listings for someone to supply them with what they want. What this means is that marketing should be quite easy for you. Just list what you offer through Gumtree, Craigslist, FaceBook and start building a client base.

These are the type of business ideas that start small but have the potential to grow on a mass scale. This is one of the reasons why I like the health industry. It falls in one of the 3 major industries that will never die, health, wealth and relationships. As long as you're somewhere in there, your business scaling opportunities are endless.

30. Affiliate Marketing

Affiliate Marketing is my bread and butter. It's the first thing that opened my eyes to making money online after losing faith in all those scammy ebooks and courses.

A friend of mine had introduced me to the idea in my last year of university and since then it had always lingered in the back of my head. I quickly put a site together, put up a product and started promoting it all over the net. After a few weeks I was making a couple of dollars a day here and there and it was amazing seeing money coming in from the online world.

3 years later and I'm doing this full-time.

Affiliate marketing is the process of promoting products for other companies and getting some commission in return. Most of it is done online and involves running traffic through your referral link to a partnered website. If people follow through with a purchase, the companies backend will pick up this came from you and will register a small commission fee for you which will be paid out to you every fortnight or month or whatever the payout term is.

There are people that make 6 figures a month doing this, even up 7 figures a month. Since the business is online, your customer potential is basically the whole internet world. You could be selling things in Spain all the way from Australia. You'll never see the product or the customer, all you do is bring in the sale and let the company do all the work.

Affiliate marketing is a great opportunity for those that want to make money while learning about marketing. Through your business life there are many realisations you will make. One of the biggest one is that NO business will grow to a sustainable point without a marketing strategy. You can't just open up a website and expect people to randomly stumble upon it. You can't just make a phone app or kindle book, upload it on to the store and expect people to buy it in masses. Sure you might get the odd visitor here and there but to grow it to a point of sustainability and stable profits, you MUST have a marketing plan. This could be as simple as paying someone on Instagram, Twitter, Facebook to post it on their page for a day or getting a blogger to send it to their email list for a small fee.

As an affiliate marketer, this is all you focus on. Sales. You don't worry about making a website or a blog or customer production or investors or any of the side distractions to business. All you worry about is sales. It's the same reason why door-to-door salesman become great businessmen, because they learn how to do the most important thing in business, get money! You're doing the same here, but on the online world.

Affiliate marketing is very broad. From paying for traffic on FaceBook and Google to running a blog like mine and selling things to people interested in what you talk about. It takes some time to read and learn about it and some more time to actually start making money with it.

The best thing about Affiliate marketing is that you can do it from anywhere around the world. All you need is an internet connection and a laptop. You may have seen pictures of people on their laptop working on a beach in some tropical island, most of them would be bloggers or internet marketers. Although you CAN live that lifestyle, most people don't because of the realities of the business. You need to be constantly researching markets, different marketing techniques and keeping up to date with trends, etc. You may find yourself working hard, very hard at the start to make it work but once you do, you can definitely cut down on the hours you spend.

In 2014, I was spending about 4-6 hours a day and made 6 figures profit. My blog can be maintained at just a few hours a week. The lifestyle does exist but both of these things had me working 12 hour days at the start. There's no way around that part of the process.

If you want to learn more about affiliate marketing, you can go to through the guides on this page to get a grasp of how it works.

Other popular blogs you can follow to learn about the industry are,

smartpassiveincome.com
charlesngo.com

Conclusion

Any of these business ideas can make you money. It's up to you to follow through with the process and stick with something until it's bringing in income. None of them are going to be an easy road you can just spend 5-10 minutes a day on, they all come with separate challenges, negatives and positives.

Business has some truths to it that need to be understood in order to achieve the goals you want. One for the truths is that business takes hard work, time and persistence. You will fail here andt there but with every failure will come learnings that will make your next idea better.

The trick is to fail quickly, in ways that you don't lose too much time and money so you learn from your mistakes real quick.

Whatever you decide to do, focus on one thing until you no longer decide it's what you want to do. A lack of focus is one of the main reasons why people don't achieve their dreams. I bet if you're primary goal was to find a part time income for the year 2016, you would achieve it. The problem is that this is so low down in our priority list that our body doesn't build the necessary habits and rituals to get you to where you want to be.

Good luck and never give up.

Mateen Soudagar

www.ingramcontent.com/pod-product-compliance
Lightning Source LLC
Chambersburg PA
CBHW061445180526
45170CB00004B/1566